Welcome to

LET'S PLAY

I spy

Easter Book

Find the objects that match the riddle

I SPY

WITH MY LITTLE EYE SOMETHING BEGGINING WITH...

Chick

I SPY

WITH MY LITTLE EYE SOMETHING BEGGINING WITH...

Ee

Egg

I SPY

WITH MY LITTLE EYE SOMETHING BEGGINING WITH...

Basket

I SPY

WITH MY LITTLE EYE SOMETHING BEGGINING WITH...

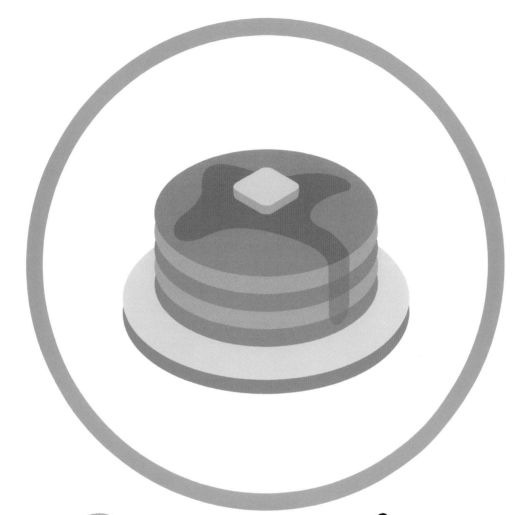

Pancake

I SPY

WITH MY LITTLE EYE SOMETHING BEGGINING WITH...

Grass

I SPY

WITH MY LITTLE EYE SOMETHING BEGGINING WITH...

Rr

Rabbit

I SPY

WITH MY LITTLE EYE SOMETHING BEGGINING WITH...

Lamb

I SPY

WITH MY LITTLE EYE SOMETHING BEGGINING WITH...

sun

I SPY

WITH MY LITTLE EYE SOMETHING BEGGINING WITH...

Kirk

I SPY

WITH MY LITTLE EYE SOMETHING
BEGGINING WITH...

Water

I SPY

WITH MY LITTLE EYE SOMETHING BEGGINING WITH...

Family

I SPY

WITH MY LITTLE EYE SOMETHING BEGGINING WITH...

yellow egg

yellow egg

I SPY

WITH MY LITTLE EYE SOMETHING BEGGINING WITH...

green egg

green egg

I SPY

WITH MY LITTLE EYE SOMETHING BEGGINING WITH...

pink egg

pink egg

I SPY

WITH MY LITTLE EYE SOMETHING BEGGINING WITH...

orange egg

orange egg

I SPY

WITH MY LITTLE EYE SOMETHING BEGGINING WITH...

violet egg

violet egg

I SPY

WITH MY LITTLE EYE SOMETHING BEGGINING WITH...

colorful egg

colorful egg

I SPY

WITH MY LITTLE EYE SOMETHING BEGGINING WITH...

chocolate egg

chocolate egg

Congratulations

you are a genius

VISIT OUR AUTHOR PAGE ON AMAZON

Printed in Great Britain
by Amazon